IN DEFENCE OF DONKEYS

IN DEFENCE OF DONKEYS

Elisabeth D. Svendsen MBE

Whittet Books

(Title page) *A summer's day at Town Barton Farm;* (on p. 6) *A satisfied resident.*

The publishers and author would like gratefully to acknowledge the following for the use of photographs in the book: Nicholas Toyne, LBIPP, Michael Greenwood, BA, *The Sunday Independent*, Roy Harrington, Mrs A. Robinson, Mr and Mrs D. Harbage, Mrs Wilkinson, Mrs D. Cade

First published 1985

Whittet Books Ltd, 113 Westbourne Grove, London W2 4UP

Design by Richard Kelly

British Library Cataloguing in Publication Data

Svendsen, Elisabeth D.
  In defence of donkeys.
  1. Donkeys
  I. Title
  636.1'8   SF361
  ISBN 0–905483–37–5

Typeset by Inforum Ltd, Portsmouth
Colour separations by Landmark
Printed and bound in Spain by Graficromo

Contents

Foreword

Elisabeth D. Svendsen is the mother of four children and a trained Froebel teacher. In recognition of her work for donkeys and handicapped children she was awarded the MBE in the New Year's Honours List in 1981. She has written books for both children and adults, this being her fourteenth, and the total sale proceeds of these go direct to the charity.

The Donkey Sanctuary is one of the most extraordinary animal rescue charities on record. As a registered charity it never refuses any donkey in need and by 1984 had taken almost 2,000 donkeys into care. Elisabeth D. Svendsen began her work of saving these gentle, intelligent, frequently mistreated creatures in 1968 and the Donkey Sanctuary charity was registered in 1973.

In addition to running the Donkey Sanctuary, she has founded two other charities: the International Donkey Protection Trust and the Slade Centre. The International Donkey Protection Trust works around the world eliminating suffering for donkeys and, we hope, helping the poor in the Third World by improving the donkeys' conditions and lengthening their lives substantially by carefully dosing to counteract parasites. The Slade Centre allows donkeys, who have been themselves rescued and brought back to full health, to help handicapped children. Every day handicapped children ride the donkeys and benefit from a loving association with them at the indoor riding school.

The Donkey Sanctuary is supported by over 52,000 subscribers, and possibly one of the reasons for its success is that it is open free to the public every day of the week, so people can see how their money is spent. Out of 144,000 registered charities in the country, the Donkey Sanctuary in 1983 was listed as the 81st largest. It has the lowest administration and fund raising overheads of any of the animal charities quoted, being only 7.2p in the £1.

This book describes the histories of ten of the donkeys that have been taken into the sanctuary for various reasons and illustrates the many sides of the charity's work. The net proceeds of the book go in total to the charity's work and we hope you will enjoy these true stories.

Aubrey and Austin

I first met Aubrey on May 9th, 1974. At this time the sanctuary was very small indeed and was run from my own small private house in Ottery St Mary. Miss Philpin, who ran a charity in Reading called 'The Helping Hand Animal Welfare League Donkey Sanctuary', had phoned me the night before to say that she had four donkeys that she just couldn't cope with, and had asked if I would take them in if she sent them down to me. Not without some trepidation, I had agreed. Of the four donkeys to arrive Aubrey was in the most reasonable condition, but his feet were very overgrown and he was a very shy and nervous donkey. He had no particular friends and tended to be the type of donkey to which I give the label 'a loner'. He was quite young, aged about three years, with a nice smooth coat of a metal grey colour, which certainly repaid brushing. Despite being so shy he appeared to appreciate greatly the loving care we gave him and we were soon able to win his confidence. However, he remained very much a single donkey until the arrival of Austin.

I had problems in trying to find names for donkeys and Aubrey was named after my father, as this was his middle name. He had visited shortly after Aubrey had arrived and had expressed such an interest in him that he became the donkey's namesake.

Later in 1974 – on June 29th – Miss Philpin, who had run the sanctuary in Reading, died and in her will she left all her donkeys to me. This meant 204 donkeys to be collected and named, and by the time I had been able to make the desperate arrangements needed to collect them all, it was mid-July. Up to this time, my son Paul had been in Reading, camping 'on site' to be with the donkeys and he already knew many of them and had given them names. Amongst a large group of 30, which we brought down in one big waggon, was the donkey that we named Austin. He was two years old and took an immediate liking to Aubrey and from that date they have remained inseparable friends.

I had thought Aubrey's feet were bad, but Austin's were quite horrific. They were extremely elongated due to the fact that they had

Aubrey and Austin in their current home.

9

not been regularly trimmed by a farrier (a job that should be done every couple of months). His walking was very, very difficult. He was most patient when the farrier visited and attended to the problem by paring down his feet, provided that Aubrey was somewhere near at hand. They soon shared the same stable and, when the donkeys were turned out into the meadows, they were always to be found together.

After the two little friends had been together for over a year they were both fully recovered, and I felt they would be better going to a home, as we allow good homes to adopt some. Having had to take so many donkeys in, I was obviously in a great deal of trouble as regards finding sufficient space for them all, and I was grateful to accept an offer of a home for both Aubrey and Austin. The home was local and was offered by a farmer who had plenty of land and was well used to dealing with livestock. As with all donkeys going out on rehabilitation, we were very careful to get forms signed to ensure that the donkeys would always remain ours, whatever happened, and also that the new owners would agree to the donkeys being visited every three months by our inspector for the area, Mr Judge. Despite having so many donkeys, I was always sad to see departures from the sanctuary, and particularly so with Aubrey and Austin, who had made such a delightful little pair and had in fact done so much for each other. However, knowing they would be in good hands, I fairly cheerfully waved them goodbye.

They were extremely happy with the farming family, and were regularly visited by Mr Judge. Then, early in 1981, the family began to have problems, they were unable to get a farrier who would call regularly enough to do the donkeys' feet, and, of course, Austin needed rather special care as our inspector had no wish for him to get back into the sort of condition he had been in. Eventually, as the farrier situation was not resolved, both Austin and Aubrey came back to the sanctuary in October 1981.

As is the case with every new arrival at the sanctuary, they had to go through the four-week isolation period to ensure they were not incubating any disease. Once this was over they were able to go out to Paccombe Farm, which is one of the sanctuary's properties just under two miles away from here. On Paccombe Farm we have an extremely good manager, Derek Battison, who has been with the sanctuary for many years. The 188 acres are mainly of grass and lie in a sheltered valley on southern facing slopes, so the donkeys have every advantage of the beautiful Devonshire weather and sunshine. A small stream runs through the farm, which provides natural watering for those donkeys who prefer it to the water from the troughs. There are very large airy barns, so that during the winter every donkey can be protected from the cold winds and rain, which can prove fatal to these animals, as they are not indigenous to this country. So many hooves cutting up the grass in winter when the ground is soft would also play havoc with our pasture management and so, for both reasons, the donkeys winter mainly indoors. All the barns are very carefully arranged and we have a special area where families go, known as Masstock Barn. This has smaller enclosures, all with their own run-out areas so that the donkeys can get fresh air and go on the hard concrete if required, as well as adequate feeding areas so that everyone can get at the feed and there is no bullying. Some donkeys tend to try to eat more than others, due to either natural greed or extra size, and the smaller members of the family always have to be protected. There is a tendency for some donkeys to eat rather too much in the winter and to put on excess weight, which can in itself become a problem. Obesity can be one of several reasons for laminitis (a foot complaint), but even more serious, for hyperlipaemia. In this condition, body fat reserves become excessive and release liquid fat into the blood vessels. This does not dissolve in the blood because blood is water-based and this liquid fat behaves like a thrombosis and chokes all the minor arteries in vital organs causing death. Rations are very carefully distributed to provide a proportion of hay, necessary to the diet, with an adequate supply of eating barley straw, which the donkeys find useful both as roughage and indeed as an occupation.

As the sanctuary grew, we were able to afford our own veterinary surgeon and, following three years of hard work and planning, we designed and developed our new hospital, which was opened in 1982. To make full use of its facilities, our veterinary team was gradually increased to four: a senior veterinary surgeon with great experience, a graduate veterinary surgeon and two RANAs, trained animal nurses. The hospital was built because the sanctuary had developed to such an extent that we had taken over 1,500 donkeys into care and donkeys requiring special treatment and operations had to be taken on the long journey to Exeter, as we had not the operating facilities nor the staff at the sanctuary.

The design of the hospital is rather unique. With our vets, I had visited animal hospitals in many parts of the country, and we had taken notes on what we considered were the best features of each unit; we carefully considered how we could incorporate these in a hospital specifically built just for donkeys. The main aim was, of course, to cut out much of the trauma experienced by animals having to be transported or moved physically from area to area and,

(Overleaf) *Austin being given his knock-down anaesthetic.*

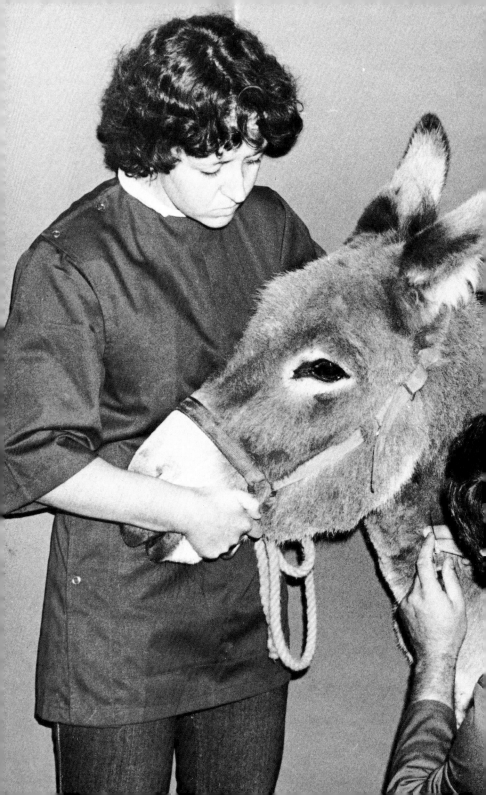

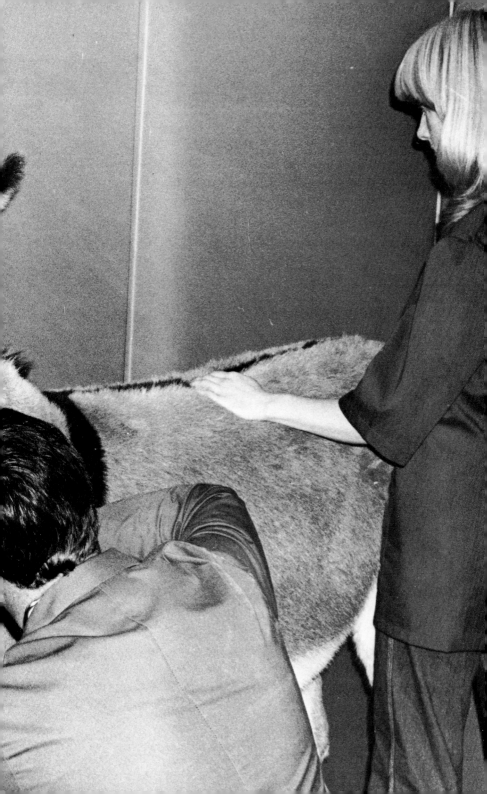

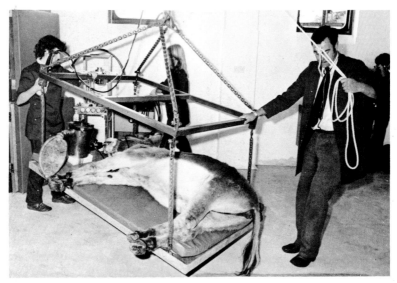

The sleeping donkey is manoeuvred into position.

with this in mind, we eventually planned our unit. We needed operating facilities, which included an operating theatre and preparation room, an X-ray unit and dark room for developing films, a recovery area and intensive-care boxes. In addition we needed laboratories so that we could regularly check both blood and dung samples to ensure the donkeys' health. It was a big project, and finally completed in 1982.

Down at Paccombe, Derek had noticed that Austin was having some difficulty in eating, and during one of the routine examinations by the veterinary surgeons, it was found that he had a very large sharp tooth which had grown and was cutting into his bottom jaw, thus causing pain when eating. It was decided to extract this difficult tooth and, in fact, Austin was the very first donkey to use the operating theatre.

As Austin and Aubrey are such close friends it was necessary to give Aubrey a sedative when Austin was given his pre-med jab at 9 a.m., as without an injection Aubrey would have fretted terribly at their parting. At 11 a.m. both animals were a bit woozy, but even then Aubrey kicked up a fuss when Austin was led out on a head-collar. Austin was then taken into a completely padded room, and whilst standing on a special pallet in the middle room, he was given a knock-down drug. It is never easy to anaesthetize a donkey. They have an extremely narrow trachea, and generally paediatric

The operating table is adjusted to the correct height; (overleaf) *the offending tooth is extracted.*

anaesthesia tubes (which are very narrow) are used to avoid any discomfort. In Austin's case, however, the tube slipped in easily, and he was connected to the anaesthetic machine whilst still lying in the knock-down box. Now soundly asleep on the pallet, Austin was attached to the overhead hoist and lifted up and gently moved to the operating theatre. The doors to the operating theatre had previously been closed, so that beforehand Austin would have had no idea that he was standing in anything other than a normal donkey box. The operating table was specially designed so that it can be moved by an electronic device higher or lower to suit the veterinary surgeon. The hoist was able to deposit Austin correctly on the table and the vet was then able to adjust the height of the table as required.

The tooth was extracted, the pallet on which Austin was still sleeping soundly was moved down a long corridor with recovery boxes on either side. The pallet holding him was gently lowered to the floor of the box and he was left safely to come round quietly. It takes several hours for donkeys to recover from an anaesthetic, and they do tend to stagger around rather. However, the padded walls ensure that there is no danger to the donkey in falling over and damaging itself, and the special leather-covered pallet, on which the donkey is gently moved to and from the operating theatre, provides a good grip for the hooves.

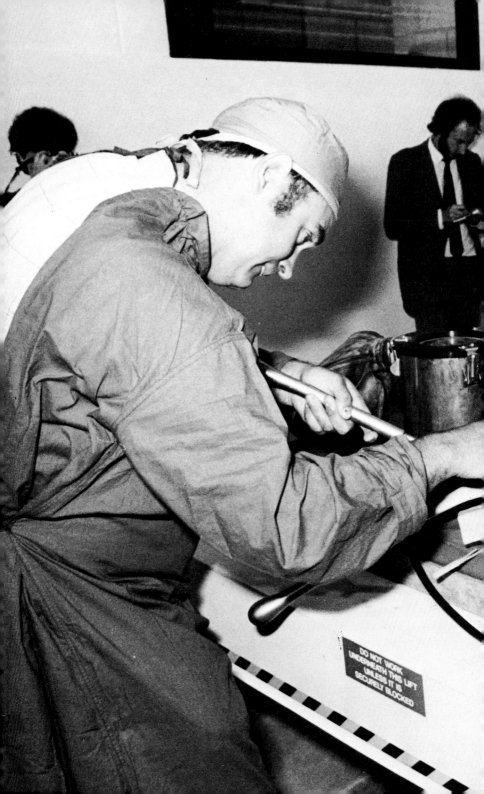

DO NOT WORK
UNDERNEATH THIS LIFT
UNLESS IT IS
SECURELY BLOCKED

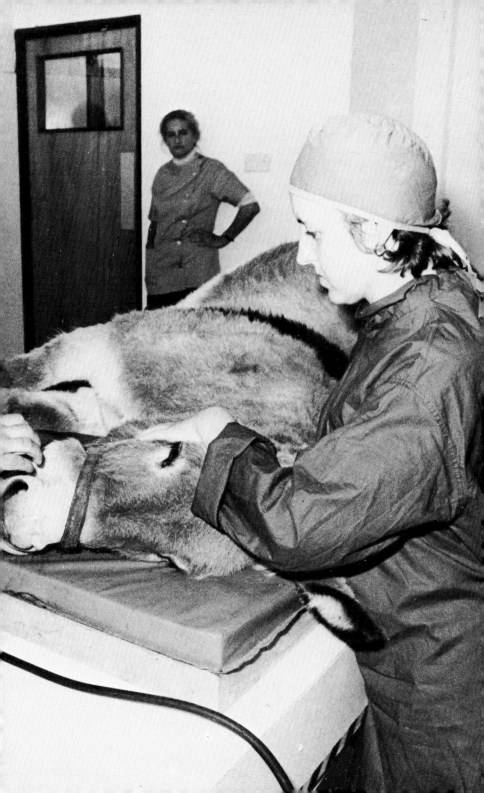

As soon as Austin was on his feet, the now quieter Aubrey was led in to join him. You would have imagined they had been away from each other for years by the vociferous welcome that Aubrey gave him, and it just proved to us how very close indeed donkey friendships become.

Shortly after Austin's recovery from his operation, an extremely good home for two donkeys was offered on Caldey Island, off Tenby in North Wales. By this time our inspectorate force had increased to six full-time and forty voluntary inspectors and it was Iwan Pritchard, our Welsh inspector, who had to go across by boat to inspect this new home that appeared so suitable. The home proved entirely satisfactory. There was plenty of grazing, excellent fencing, sufficient water and adequate stabling for the donkeys in inclement weather or if it was very hot and sunny and they needed to get away from the flies. There were plenty of children, as the new home was next to the village school, and the most detailed arrangements were made so that Austin and Aubrey could travel across to their new home by boat with the minimum of stress.

It appeared that the whole island turned out to see their arrival and they have really settled down there very well. It is not perhaps the easiest place for our inspector to visit and I would like to quote a small section from Iwan Pritchard's report received in September 1983:

> Drove to Tenby, had a very rough crossing, boats were very busy, had to wait until 4 p.m. for a crossing. Went to see the donkeys and attend to their needs. Worming and foot trimming, etc. Failed to get back as a force 11 gale blew up and the last boat due at 6 p.m. failed to get across. Stayed overnight at the Caldey Guest House and it was 1 p.m. the next day before a boat made it across the water. The gale was still in full force. The crossing normally takes 20 minutes but it took 1 hour 10 minutes to get back, and all hands had to man the pumps to stay afloat as the waves were breaking over the bows. By jove, there is variety in our work! We were in good hands as Alan Thomas, the boatman, is also the Tenby lifeboat cox.

Today Aubrey and Austin are still very happily settled, and we hope that they will be able to stay in this good home for many, many more years. It is surprising that donkeys can in fact live up to the age of fifty perfectly healthily, and we sincerely hope that this will be the case for both Aubrey and Austin.

Crackers

Much of our work would be totally impossible without the continued support of the general public. Not only do we rely on them for funds, but we also rely on them to help us in our constant job of rescuing donkeys from trouble in all parts of the country. From a member of the public we first heard of the desperate plight of a little donkey who, because we rescued him at Christmas, we have called 'Crackers'. We know very little of Crackers's early background, but we do know that at the age of two he found himself tethered to a stake on some waste land in the north of England in early November 1983. The length of the rope by which he was tethered was short and the amount of grazing available was almost nil. The weather was desperately cold, wet and windy, the very worst conditions to which a donkey can be subjected. In desperation, Crackers eventually managed to break free of his tether but, in doing so, inflicted a deep wound from the post on the inside of his hind legs. He then began to wander, looking for food, and apparently was seen for six weeks at various times, wandering around the small northern town, stopping the traffic on more than one occasion; reports were made both to the police and the RSPCA, but neither was able to find the donkey. Eventually, being terrified of the traffic and near to death, he returned to within a mile of the waste ground where he had originally been tethered and here his luck changed. He lay exhausted outside the house of a member of the public who fortunately was not only a caring animal lover, but was also determined to do something about his pitiful condition. Giving him a feed of hay, she then rang the RSPCA, who in turn contacted the Donkey Sanctuary inspectors.

The story told over the telephone was almost unbelievable: the weather was about freezing, there was a light covering of snow on the fields, and more was forecast. The inspectors realized the gravity of the situation and immediately postponed the private arrangements they had made, and drove as quickly as possible to the area. They arrived within two hours of the call on Friday, December 9th. To say they were appalled was an understatement. Their experienced eyes told them how bad things were and, without

The wasteland where Crackers was found.

a word, one of them climbed back in the car and drove back to get the donkey trailer. Very gently Crackers was loaded in and, supported by straps, he managed the journey to their house; I'm sure you can imagine his feelings when put into a warm stable, with deep straw, clear fresh water and a small warm feed of bran, oats and molasses, the first real meal he had received in many weeks.

He was found to be in a terrible condition and, following a telephone call to headquarters, it was agreed that a local vet be called in immediately for all the treatment necessary. This started before any attempt was made to move him. The local veterinary surgeon found that Crackers was suffering from very bad anaemia, had lung noises which he said were probably due to a previous bout of pneumonia which had not been treated; and a very, very bad wound on the hind leg which had now turned septic, sustained while escaping from his tether. In addition to this, he had an injury on the left eye, which had left it misted, and he was full of worms and lice.

Almost all the Donkey Sanctuary Voluntary Inspectors (of which there are over forty) are members of the Donkey Breed Society. This means that they have a great interest in donkeys and have experience of all sides of donkey welfare from the showing and breeding of donkeys to the special care of donkeys. These voluntary inspectors can immediately follow up any calls for help on any problem affecting donkeys. They advise on suitable homes, general donkey welfare and feeding, and visit all our rehabilitation donkeys on a regular basis. To back them up we have a team of six full-time inspectors. Without exception these highly skilled men have either been employed by the RSPCA or the British Horse Society and all are extremely knowledgeable not only on donkey and mule needs but also on the law relating to all aspects of misuse of animals. We give a seven-day service, twenty-four hours a day, and it is fair to say that all those employed are totally dedicated to their task. This was proved beyond any doubt in the case of Crackers, who needed almost full-time nursing right through Christmas for nearly five weeks before he was declared fit by the veterinary surgeon to travel down to the sanctuary. For Crackers, he must have felt he was in heaven. Once he had got over his tetanus and antibiotic injections he was given special vitamin tablets, wormed, de-loused and had his hooves trimmed properly. Gradually, his feed was increased until he was eating ad-lib hay and two meals of bran, flaked maize and oats a day. Every night he was rugged to make sure he lost no body heat and energy, so desperately needed in his fight for survival during those early days.

There is no doubt that the loving care he received enabled him to make a miraculous return to health, and what surprised everybody was the immense friendliness of this little stallion, who had received such bad treatment previously at the hands of human beings. When Perry, the driver, arrived to pick him up to take him back to the sanctuary, he was greeted with the most unusual reception on his arrival. Normally, our inspectors are very pleased when our lorry arrives to pick up the animals they have rescued to take them back to the sanctuary, but in this particular case, such a bond of affection had sprung up that there were almost tears at the parting. Crackers was loaded extremely carefully into the new sanctuary lorry. We have designed this specially and, by placing the special padded sections to the positions required, we can provide a safe, comfortable travelling area for the donkey, padded on three sides and with a good supply of hay and water available on the fourth side. Crackers was also rugged up with the rugs provided for travelling donkeys and the long journey back to the sanctuary began on January 13th. Perry, the driver, must be the most qualified person in the world for travelling donkeys. Perry has loaded and carried most of the 1,800 donkeys received in to the sanctuary; he drives very slowly with his precious cargoes, stopping every hour to get in with the donkey to talk to it and make sure it has adequate water and hay. When Crackers arrived at the sanctuary he found a great welcome waiting for him. A box had been prepared for him in the Hospital Block, as

(Overleaf) *Crackers outside the Slade Centre.*

Crackers shortly after arrival at the sanctuary.

we knew he would still need special treatment for some time to come. We couldn't believe how small he was when the big ramp of the lorry was opened and the little broken-coloured donkey's figure appeared at the top. He was still limping badly from the wound, although it was now no longer septic, and giving him less trouble. But despite this, having looked around the top of the ramp, he gave a large bray of joy before walking down to join us all. Despite his five weeks' care he was still pathetically thin and his head seemed far too big for his body. Gently he was led into the stable and no doubt he was delighted to see he had the same facilities as he had had at his previous stabling. As all donkeys do, he wandered slowly round the box, sniffing and nuzzling at everything until he was quite satisfied he knew exactly where he was. Then he came back to the door and put his head over to be petted and loved. Fortunately Crackers had been given all his anti-tetanus and 'flu injections up north, so he had no nasty treatment in the hospital. At the sanctuary every donkey has an annual 'flu injection. This protects them against the very contagious equine 'flu, one of our biggest dangers with so many donkeys together. Tetanus is also a risk and they have an injection every two years against this.

Being a stallion he could not be mixed with any of the other new donkey arrivals and, in any event, he was not well enough at this stage to even compete on a friendly basis for food. As he spent a great deal of his time either having to stand still or lying down with the pain in his leg, infra-red lamps were fixed up for him to keep him warm and each day he was taken for a short walk to keep his leg exercised.

Shortly after his arrival another little stallion called Daniel Chestnut came in and was put next door to Crackers, and round the stable doors these two began to make firm friends. After six weeks it was decided that Crackers was fit to stand the castration operation which both our veterinary surgeons strongly advised, as they felt his recovery could then continue without interruption. Crackers was castrated on the same day as Daniel Chestnut and both the donkeys were then placed together to recover and make friends. Crackers's improvement continued at an even faster pace once he had a friend. A very special bond quickly developed as they recovered from their operations together. Crackers really enjoyed being groomed, obviously a pleasure he had never experienced before. He never fidgeted, no matter how many times the same area was brushed, and at times leant on the groomer more and more heavily, eyes half shut and obviously enjoying every second. He soon trained Daniel into the donkey friendship act known as 'mutual grooming': they would stand for hours, head to tail, grooming each other's hair with their teeth. When they had both been passed as fit and sound by the veterinary staff, a big decision had to be made. Daniel was earmarked for the Slade Centre, but due to Crackers's malnutrition, eye damage and chronic lung problem, he would never be fit to join the crème de la crème. It was also obvious, however, that they could not be split and Crackers himself solved the problem by joining Daniel as the 'petting' donkey at the Slade Centre, not to give rides to the children, but just to be loved and petted, as this seems to be the one thing that Crackers really wants.

Being what we call a 'broken coloured' donkey, Crackers is very attractive, and, in view of his delight at being with children, we have decided that he can go on the 'adoption' list we have specially for schools. Here the children take a special interest in a specific donkey and we provide pictures and information for them. Collections are made and the children love to feel they can associate with one special donkey. Local schools love to visit and of course the main object of attraction is the school's 'own' donkey. Throughout the country our staff lecture and give film shows for children in schools,

(Overleaf) *Crackers and his friends happily grazing.*

and the lesson on the donkey which this includes will, we hope, ensure a better educated next generation when it comes to donkeys' needs. Because of his name, it was felt that a new story book for children could be written, and so *Eeyore and Christmas Crackers* has been published. By both these means, Crackers will be a great help in the funding of the sanctuary, as many schools will help us in financing his upkeep, and all the proceeds of the book help to feed the ever-increasing number of mouths.

Crackers's future life is now assured. Enquiries in the area in which he was found have failed to produce the owner, despite the police being informed and, should the owner ever turn up to claim Crackers, he could face a prosecution for direct cruelty, so it would seem Crackers will remain with the sanctuary; we hope he will have a trouble-free life ahead of him.

Daniel Chestnut

Donkeys come into the sanctuary for various reasons, and many of them have the most interesting previous histories; these are always taken into account when we decide if it is in the best interests of the animal for it to come into the sanctuary. The owner of Daniel Chestnut had certainly had his share of misfortunes. Despite being a cripple and being permanently confined to a wheelchair, Mr Bellamy had managed to cope not only with Daniel but also with driving horses; he had always loved his animals dearly. As well as having a handicapped son, his wife was taken ill, and sadly they then had to agree that Daniel Chestnut should be taken into care. Mr Bellamy personally told us the most delightful story of Daniel Chestnut.

Apparently, Daniel was born in Worcester, where his donkey family must have been companions to horses. It is well known amongst horse and donkey owners that even the most lively horse can be quietened by the companionship of a donkey, the two species generally getting on well together. There are stories of very well known racehorses who always have to have a donkey with them when they travel; a badly injured racehorse in the Exeter area had one of our donkeys as a stable companion for six months while its broken leg healed, the two becoming almost inseparable friends. One of the problems of keeping donkeys and horses together is that unfortunately the donkey can be a silent carrier of a parasite called lungworm. The donkey apparently is not really affected by this parasite as it isn't expected to extend itself to galloping, trotting, etc., and so therefore shows very few symptoms. However, in the horse it is a very different story and damage to the lungs can make the horse almost useless to its owner. A great deal of work has been done on this recently and we are now able to say with confidence that the treatment we carry out on our donkeys cures them and prevents them from being carriers, so they may be accepted by horse owners as perfect companions for their animals. Treatment of both donkeys and horses should be done regularly under the supervision of the local vet.

Daniel lost his mother before he was properly weaned and so he decided that his mother was instead a 16-hand bay mare who also

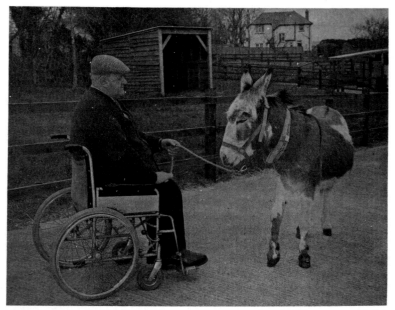

Daniel Chestnut with Mr Bellamy; (opposite) *Daniel Chestnut with his precious load.*

had a foal. Daniel got quite used to suckling and the horse mare was quite happy to allow this to happen. Unfortunately, the horse was sold and one day was put in a horse box to be taken away. In a complete panic, seeing his milk ration leaving, Daniel managed to leap through the fence and galloped after the horse box. Luckily, a police patrol car was nearby and the horse box was stopped, Daniel loaded onto the box and driven back to the farm. He was then put in a small shed with a window and the horse box set off once again with the foster mother. With one great leap, Daniel leapt through the plate glass window and once again galloped after the box. Realizing the tremendous distress to both the donkey and the horse mare, the new owner took pity on Daniel and he was put in the horse box and taken away with his 'horse' mother. His new owner, Mr Bellamy, weaned little Daniel as soon as possible, looking after him very carefully and putting up with continuous braying day and night for two days before Daniel finally accepted he was a donkey and quite old enough to eat his own food.

As Mr Bellamy had always been interested in driving, he decided to train Daniel to pull a small cart. With this end in view, the Bellamys spent many hours walking with him, leading him along

quiet lanes to overcome natural hazards, and gradually introducing him to traffic. The walks took the form of a game and were enjoyed by all. By the time Daniel was two years old he was introduced to long reining, and by three years old was quite happy to feel a harness on his back and a bridle with bit in his mouth. A donkey does not mature fully until the age of four, so should not be worked earlier. When he was four years old he pulled a small log attached to a harness for the first time. To Daniel this was a great event, and fortunately, when he felt the pull of the log, his normal instinct was to stand still and think for a moment and this gave time for Mr Bellamy to reassure him. Soon he was gently encouraged to 'walk on', which he did, dragging the log behind him. Sometimes, Mr Bellamy pulled the harness from the front, and Daniel learnt not to panic when he felt the breaching pull up tight on his back legs. This helped him greatly later going down hill with a trap.

Eventually, he was ready to try the trap. Mr Bellamy had built a very light one for him, running on two bicycle wheels. Patiently, Daniel was broken in, and he got used to voice commands as well as the shake of the reins and the gentle touch of the driving whip on his back.

Daniel was left as an entire donkey, or, as we would know it, a stallion. Despite this, his temperament stayed extremely good and gentle, quite unusual when a donkey has not been gelded and when he became six years old, he was used to cover two donkey mares. Unfortunately disaster struck one of the mares when she was eight months pregnant. A large black 16-hand stallion was put in the next field and one day the horse managed to get over the concrete wall and attacked the jenny (the name for a female donkey). Daniel bravely defended both himself and the jenny but both were fairly badly injured, the jenny so severely that she had to be put to sleep. But Daniel managed to survive even though he was bitten several times. Fortunately, the other jenny was all right and eventually gave birth to a filly exactly the same colour as Daniel.

Daniel's other meeting with a horse was at the Chelwood Horse Show. Horses do not always take kindly to donkeys and unfortunately at the show, when the judge was just walking round the hunters after their saddles had been taken off, Daniel decided to bray loudly. This caused a tremendous commotion among the horses, who reared up, kicked out and caused a near disaster. Daniel quite enjoyed it but Mr Bellamy was told to remove the donkey and not bring it back again.

Fortunately, Daniel was much more popular at the many fêtes he attended, and he thoroughly enjoyed giving rides; the 10 pences he collected went to charity and he raised over £500 for children's organizations in Bristol.

When Mrs Bellamy was suddenly taken ill and had to go to hospital, the Bellamys decided very sadly that Daniel had to come into the sanctuary but they sent him in with one specific wish, and that was that he should be allowed to help in the Slade Centre run from the Donkey Sanctuary here.

When Daniel arrived in the sanctuary, being a stallion, of course he had to be castrated. No donkey can remain entire for various reasons – one being the temperament problem with stallions and another the fact that very soon all the mares in the sanctuary would become pregnant. The donkeys to be castrated first undergo their four-week isolation period and during this time are paired up with another friend. In this case Daniel's friend was Crackers, whose story precedes this one. After staying six weeks both Daniel and Crackers were castrated on the same day. Thanks to the hospital facilities the donkeys were subjected to the minimum stress. As far as they were concerned, the worst problem was no food the previous evening. As with humans, it is very dangerous to anaesthetize a donkey with a full stomach and so from 5 p.m. the night before the donkeys have to be starved. In addition, peat bedding is used instead of straw, as many donkeys enjoy straw and will eat their bedding. However, a tranquillizer early on the appointed day stopped their worries and by tea time the two friends were able to tuck into a good meal in the Hospital Recovery Wing. After a further four weeks the two donkeys were allocated to the Slade Centre, Cracker's role to be a petting and loving donkey, rather than a riding donkey.

The Slade Centre for handicapped children actually started in 1975. Before we had a special building, we used to take a selected group of well trained donkeys out to handicapped schools in the Exeter area; the results were so wonderful that after a lot of effort we were able to raise sufficient funds to build a large indoor riding centre where the children can come every day of the year, winter and summer. The donkeys are selected for the centre very carefully indeed. They must be in first-class condition, love children and giving rides, and some are trained for driving. Normally the team consists of twenty donkeys, each of which is an individual in its own right. Alfred is the longest serving member and is a very large donkey with an extremely gentle nature. As the children arrive in the specially adapted ambulance/coach from their hospitals and schools within a 25-mile radius, those donkeys not already tacked up and waiting trot to the railings of their field and then watch as the children are unloaded and taken to the centre. They all enjoy the

(Overleaf) *Daniel on duty pulling the cart.*

work and Daniel was no exception. As soon as he had recovered it was decided to try him in the Slade Centre. From the moment he went in through the big doors to the main arena, it was quite obvious that Daniel had a love of children. A big strong donkey, and already trained to the cart, he was absolutely ideal. The majority of the children attending are able to have normal rides on the donkeys, but unfortunately some are so severely handicapped that they can only ride either propped on the long seat of the donkey cart, or actually be pushed in their wheelchairs up into the specially adapted cart, which allows them to drive from their wheelchairs. This was the cart to which Daniel was allocated. His past training was immediately apparent and also the way he enjoyed the job. He quickly became a favourite with all the children, who would shout for Daniel when they first came into the centre, and his consistent good temper has made him a marvellous acquisition.

Daniel is an unusual donkey in many ways. Normally a stallion who is gelded so late retains many difficult behavioural problems. Daniel seems to have coped admirably with these, and his energy is channelled solely into his work. The children can safely love and pet him and he enjoys all the attention. His early training obviously played a large part in his suitability for the job, and the fact that his owners really loved him so well has contributed to this delightful result.

Mr Bellamy and family continue to take a great interest in Daniel, and indeed have contributed financially towards his stay with us. In view of our permanent financial difficulties this help has been much appreciated by us. We look forward to Mr Bellamy coming to see Daniel in his new role at the Slade Centre and we know he will be as delighted as we are to see that his good early training has paid such dividends to so many poor handicapped children.

Muffin

Generally, donkeys make ideal pets, being placid in nature, intelligent and easily trainable and with a natural love of children which has been appreciated for many, many years. Unfortunately, there are occasional exceptions, and one of the donkeys to come into the sanctuary, called Muffin, has been just such an exception.

Muffin was born in Yorkshire in April 1968. He was a very strong little foal, a beautiful chocolate brown colour, and by the time he was five months old his owners decided to sell him. A local family heard of the donkey for sale and, as they had adequate land and a small stable, decided they would purchase him. So far as Muffin was concerned his life changed very drastically the day he was loaded into the back of a van and driven some miles to his new home. At this time he had not been castrated and he had already begun to develop stallion tendencies. His new owners previously had little experience of donkeys, with the exception of seaside rides for the children and an old donkey whom they had known quite well belonging to a friend of theirs. Muffin took them completely by surprise. They had expected a gentle, docile pet but instead, even at this early age, they found themselves faced with a problem. Try as they might to include him in family gatherings, Muffin generally seemed to have other ideas. The first sign of real trouble came when on one of his frequent visits in and out of the house, as the garden gate was often left open for this purpose, he turned round and kicked his new owner quite deliberately and with astounding accuracy. After this his visits into the house were stopped and Muffin lived in the field adjoining. Alongside the field was a main road and Muffin soon found that he could gain attention by braying loudly over the wall and local people began to come up and bring their children with them to give him tit-bits and feed him. Very soon Muffin began to expect everybody who came up to the wall to feed him and after various complaints from people who had their fingers bitten when just reaching out to stroke him, his owners built a retaining fence to stop him getting up to the wall. By this time

(Overleaf) *Muffin fit and ready for action.*

Muffin was obviously very lonely. The children were small and when they came into the field to try to play with Muffin he always got too boisterous or vigorous and each visit seemed to terminate in yet more disaster. The family had three goats whom they felt would be companions for Muffin but Muffin got more and more difficult to handle and even chased and bit the goats, so that he ended up alone again in his paddock. In the hope of making him more placid, he was castrated by the local vet when he was 1½ years old.

Mr Tetley, the father of the family, determined to try and solve the situation by training and both he and a friend of the family spent many hours trying to persuade Muffin to walk and trot on command and to accept a small felt saddle to give the children rides. The family were well aware that donkeys cannot carry more than eight stone in weight and only the smallest children were allowed to ride when Muffin had reached the age of three, still too early for the donkey's back to bear a weight over 6 stone. Unfortunately, he became even more difficult to handle and the attempts at training terminated when Mr Tetley took him to the local agricultural show at Keighley. There was a donkey class and he decided that the good behaviour of other donkeys would set Muffin a good example, and he would settle down and become the pet the family all hoped for. However, unfortunately for both Mr Tetley and the judge, Muffin did not agree. To try and get rid of some of his high spirits, Mr Tetley walked him all the way to the show and perhaps everything would have been well if the show had started on time. But, due to delays, Muffin had had time to recharge his batteries by the time he was due to go in the ring. He walked round quite quietly with Mr Tetley, but when asked to trot the length of the ring so that the judge could observe him, both Mr Tetley and Muffin landed up in the crowds and it took many willing hands to help them back into the ring again. The final disaster came when the judge inspected the mouth to check that the teeth were all in order and there was no sign of parrot mouth (a fairly common occurrence in many donkeys where either the lower or upper jaw is set so far back that the teeth do not meet properly) and Muffin made a very determined attempt to 'bite the hand that judged him'. Mr Tetley said it was not one of his better days and, as was to be expected, Muffin did not even get placed.

By this time, the family were beginning to feel an acute sense of failure and wondered whether they should get another donkey to keep Muffin company, but Mrs Tetley was so worried about even going into the field with Muffin that she didn't feel they dared risk this. As the children got older they used to regularly have chases in Muffin's field and one day they left the gate open and Muffin decided to investigate the local village. After spending almost two hours leading half the village a dance, he was eventually restrained by four young men and returned to his field. After having Muffin for twelve years and realizing how very little pleasure they had obtained from him, the Tetleys finally decided to send him to the sanctuary after a particularly vicious incident where Mrs Tetley was almost savaged whilst trying to pass to milk the goats. The family had had enough but still they didn't want to see Muffin get into any more trouble. Through Maurice Clare, a voluntary inspector of the Donkey Sanctuary, they had heard of our work and so it was decided that for both the safety of the family and for Muffin's future, he should be sent to the sanctuary.

The instructions to our driver were quite clear. Written on the intake sheet he was told that on no account should he turn his back to the animal. We were all ready for him when he arrived at the sanctuary and he was handled with the care he deserved following his history. As he was a gelding, it was not essential to keep him separated from other donkeys when he arrived and so he was able to be quarantined in a small group of five, during which time he was handled consistently and professionally many times a day. The first job that we had to do was to gain his confidence and also to show him that he couldn't get away with any bad behaviour and that both biting and kicking were not acceptable if he was to fit into a herd of donkeys. Great care was taken when approaching him in his group and it was noticeable that his first approach was always with lips curled back and teeth bared, the proffered hand being in imminent danger of a firm bite. By placing one hand under his chin and one hand over his nose it was possible to talk to him quietly while stroking him and standing so close to his side that he was unable to turn and kick. Apart from the skilled administration of the veterinary staff, I was able to spend a fair amount of time with him in the group in the evenings after the routine office work was finished and began to feel at least a little progress had been made by the time his period at Slade House Farm was over and he was ready to go out to one of the five farms for permanent settlement.

Brookfield Farm was the second farm to be purchased by the sanctuary. Charlie Courtney was appointed the manager. He had trained at Bicton Agricultural College and had spent almost two years with us getting to know donkeys. As well as being very competent, Charlie has a great love of animals and knows each of his charges not only by name but by nature; he can predict behaviour patterns of certain donkeys with astounding accuracy. The farm is fairly exposed, built on a hillside, but all 127 acres consist of the type of grassland enjoyed by donkeys and here Muffin went in November 1982. It appeared to everybody that, whilst needing the company of other donkeys, because he was so strong and tended to use his hooves so much, he would be better in what is known as 'Boys Group'. This is a group of approximately fifty geldings with a very definite pecking order already established in the group. Head of the group was a donkey with a hump back known as Treacle and for five years there was no doubt who was boss of the section. All new arrivals to the group had to conform to his close inspection; having made the new donkey's acquaintance, Treacle would either walk away, which indicated that the new donkey could join the group as an accepted member, or a small fight would ensue, our staff always being on hand to separate if things got too bad.

In this instance, neither Treacle nor Muffin saw eye to eye and both had to be separated within five minutes of meeting. Muffin then spent the next two days in a most unsettled state. Instead of gradually being accepted by the herd, he seemed to have no interest in any of the donkeys at all and was almost always to be found standing quietly on his own in a corner or outside in the run-out yards, preferring that to the company of the others. The story was very different when one of the staff went in, and Muffin would always rush to have human company in preference to donkey company. Always his mouth was wide open and there was a danger of being bitten, although by now Muffin had learned never to turn his back and kick and was relatively easy to handle. A gentle pat from the staff, a stroke and few words, and he seemed happy to trot round after them whilst they were in the big barn working. After five days, Charlie, the manager, decided to move Muffin as he obviously was not settling and by now Treacle would have nothing at all to do with him. He was moved to a mixed group including mares as well as geldings and here for the first time we found a new side to Muffin. Though he had no time at all for geldings, mares were a completely different proposition, and within hours he was extremely happily settled into the group, always being found next to a mare both for feeding and exercise, never choosing the company of a male. It is most probable that Muffin had been weaned too young and those early years without another companion and without his mother had a detrimental effect on his whole character. We were most interested to see his behaviour when the donkeys were turned out that first spring.

Each farm has to be managed very carefully to get the maximum amount of grass as of course the sanctuary relies on the grass not only for grazing but also for haymaking, and we try to make as much hay as possible to feed all the animals. Another big problem for the sanctuary in grass management is the control of parasites. All donkeys have parasites which affect both the stomachs of the donkeys and their lungs. By worming the donkeys regularly, and particularly before they go out to graze, and by a method of running sheep through the grass in rotation with the donkeys, we are able to maintain a very low level of parasitic infection. In 1983 the donkeys were turned out in May and to our joy and delight, Muffin, by now settled completely, was able to enjoy the whole summer out at grass.

Although Muffin has settled now, Charlie will tell you that any time you walk into a field where Muffin is grazing, he will immediately look up and trot over importantly to meet whoever is coming in. He still looks for tit-bits and one still has to watch one's hands, but the tendency to bite has now almost completely gone. It had seemed that Muffin could never be rehabilitated to a new home but in recent times he has improved so tremendously that it could just be possible sometime in the future. But please, if ever you think of giving a donkey a tit-bit, do think of the possible consequences for the donkey's future welfare.

Sue and Cindy

One wet Saturday afternoon, I was working quietly in the office trying to clear up some of the paperwork that tends to accumulate during a very busy donkey week. To avoid being disturbed too often we have an ansaphone connected to our telephone at evenings and weekends and I almost let the phone continue ringing when it started that particular day. However, I did pick it up to make sure that it wasn't the case of a donkey in trouble and I am very pleased indeed that I did. The news I received was most disturbing. A member of the public on a train between two small stations in the north of England had noticed two donkeys in an open field alongside the railway line with no apparent shelter. The feet of both donkeys appeared most abnormal, having curled up and, as she described them to me, 'looking more like moccasins than donkey feet'. She couldn't give me exact directions of where the donkeys were to be found, nor had she any idea to whom they belonged, but appeared quite confident that we would be able to cope with the problem. I assured her that we would do our best, and, having taken her name and address, I immediately rang our nearest inspector up in the north.

The Donkey Sanctuary always tries to get out to any complaint within twenty-four hours, and our inspector there decided this was to be no exception. Having thought the matter over he decided probably the best way to try and trace the donkeys would be to walk along the railway line between the two stations mentioned; having first obtained permission from British Rail, he set forth to trudge the four miles searching for the donkeys. The weather conditions certainly did not help him on that particular day but he was still most disappointed to arrive at the next station on the track having seen no sign of the donkeys during his walk. He rang me that evening and I gave him the complainant's telephone number so that he could get in touch with her. The following day the complainant walked with our inspector along the railway track and, recognizing sections of the landscape, was able to isolate the field where she had seen the donkeys and this time in the far corner of the field against the fence were the two donkeys in question. There was no doubt this complaint had not been exaggerated and the inspector was quite horrified to see that the feet were not only extremely long and twisted but had also rotted to a large extent. The mare was obviously in foal and very, very lame and the other smaller donkey with her was a stallion and appeared to be her son. The conditions of the land on which he found the donkeys was extremely bad, most of the land was under water and, apart from a few trees, there was no shelter at all. He had a good look around the field but could see no sign of any feed having been given to the donkeys although there was a water supply.

It took the inspector two days to trace the owner of the animals, who turned out to be a recluse. Our inspector did his best to explain the situation but the owner became extremely agitated and then even turned violent when he was told that the donkeys should be removed. Our voluntary inspector then withdrew and rang Jack Turnell, one of our chief inspectors. After further discussion the owner agreed to have the donkeys' feet attended to but, not relying on this completely, Jack Turnell drove to the field some days later and was absolutely appalled to find that the donkeys' hooves were in an almost worse condition, the owner having obviously obtained a saw and tried to cut off the growth himself. The situation was now critical, both the donkeys were in terrible trouble and in need of immediate care and attention and our inspector went straight back to the owner, very determined indeed to solve the situation.

He did not meet with a good reception; the owner, shouting and arguing and even threatening physical action, became more and more difficult. Our inspector quietly pointed out that under the circumstances he felt there were grounds for a prosecution and he felt he had no option but to call in the local police and a veterinary surgeon, and to have the donkeys removed immediately. This had the desired effect and suddenly the relinquishment form which would make the mare sanctuary property was signed. Not without some effort, our inspector managed to place the smaller donkey in a good home locally where he would receive the attention he required. In view of the mare's serious condition it was decided not to travel her the long distance down to Devon, and our voluntary inspector took her into his home so that she could get veterinary attention, be seen by a qualified farrier and allowed to recover.

As soon as she was fit to travel, our specially equipped lorry arrived to collect her. Great care was taken when loading the mare, whom we named Sue, and she was put in a special padded box with a support strap to help her keep her balance. Perry drove the lorry very slowly, with frequent stops to check that she was all right and water her. I was so pleased to see them arrive in early evening, as I had been concerned about Sue and was longing to see her for myself.

What a gentle donkey she turned out to be. She was obviously still in some discomfort from her feet and the fact that she was pregnant played no small part in this discomfort. She had not been properly fed for some time before our inspector took her in and her coat, despite the attention it had received during the last three weeks, was still very dull and lank and the donkey herself had almost no energy. After her isolation period, Sue was given a box next door to an elderly mare for company. Her feet were still giving her problems and movement was very difficult. Although she was now safe there were still very hard times ahead.

Our farrier attended her on a weekly basis and she was included on veterinary rounds every day. I spent a lot of time with her as I knew if she was going to have problems, I had to have her complete confidence at foaling time or she would not let anyone help. When her time came near she was moved into a large airy foaling box and the straw bedding was doubled every morning and evening. We were expecting trouble for three main reasons. Firstly, her son had not been fully developed himself when he had served her and very little is known as yet about the dangers of this. Secondly, any hereditary defects he had inherited from his mother could be multiplied by the incestuous relationship, and thirdly, she was in such a poor condition. We were unable to tell exactly how long she had been pregnant; the gestation period for a donkey can be anything from 9½ to 13 months and very little indication indeed is given when the foal is actually due. From my experience I have found that the donkey's udder which has been developing gradually during the pregnancy, suddenly swells dramatically about twenty-two days before the event. This is called 'springing an udder'. Careful observation will then show the actual teats swelling and turning in rather. In the last twenty-four hours we sometimes actually see waxy drops emerging, the prelude to milk and sign of imminent birth. The donkey much prefers to foal on its own and in fact will retard the birth if people are present. Almost all the donkeys born in the sanctuary have been born during the night and we try to respect the donkey's privacy, providing that we are fairly sure that all will go well. From my experience I would say that in 95% of cases this is so, but when things do go wrong, unless you are there, you are very likely to lose both mare and foal. To help with this predicament the foaling box that Sue was in had a special viewing window about 12ft high on the wall. A special staircase gave access to this and not only myself but members of the staff crept up at

Sue and Cindy, 1984.

Sue with Cindy at two days old.

frequent intervals to look through the peep-hole to make sure all was well.

Normally the birth itself takes approximately half an hour. The foal should arrive with the front legs first and the head tucked almost between them. The foal is totally enclosed in a tight mucous membrane, almost like a plastic shopping bag, but, providing the mother is fairly fit and well she will very quickly nip this open and this, plus the foal's struggles, soon splits it apart and the little foal is exposed. Both myself and the vet had made frequent visits to Sue on the night the foal was born. I had been in at 2 a.m. and Sue was standing happily chewing with no apparent sign of birth being imminent. When I next peeped through the hole at 4 in the morning, I was delightfully surprised to find her licking the small shivering wet foal which she had already extricated from the membrane.

At this time it is fairly safe to go into the donkey, as long as one

Cindy at one week old.

does not distress it, just to check that all is well with both mother and baby. There was no problem at all here. Sue was happily licking the foal and we didn't need to use the trick of rubbing a little salt on the foal's coat, which can often be a help when you get a mother who does not wish to take her offspring. I am always fascinated to see that each little hoof is carefully protected with a white rubbery material, which peels off within a few hours of the donkey's birth. This is to prevent the sharp little hooves of the foal injuring the mother either during the pregnancy or the birth itself. Having checked to the best of my knowledge that both mother and foal were well, I immediately rang the vet, who came down and pronounced everything most satisfactory. I think we were all extremely relieved, we had thought we could have a problem in the foaling, but this strong delightful little filly was in no need of anybody's help.

Sue was given a bran mash and allowed to rest quietly for the

whole of the following day. I watched with great pleasure as Cindy, as we called the little foal, staggered around on her spindly looking legs trying to find her balance. The donkey foal is one of the few young animals who does not appear to instinctively know where the udder is to be found and very often a little help is required before the suckling can commence. In this case, I was able to assist both mother and foal in completing the natural cycle and the pleasure of hearing the noisy suckling was more than reward for the last seven nights of disturbed sleep. On her first day out Cindy delighted the many visitors to the sanctuary by prancing around her mother, sometimes on all four legs rather like a young lamb, and one visitor was absolutely unable to resist her charms. She came into my office saying, 'I don't mind what it costs, Mrs Svendsen. I want to pay for the upkeep of this little donkey for life.' You can imagine how I felt; funds are always hard to get here, it does seem a constant struggle, and to have somebody offering to keep little Cindy for the rest of her natural life was almost too much. I am afraid tears came into my eyes as I thanked this wonderful person.

Sue and Cindy are now living happily together in the sanctuary. Sue's feet still continue to give her a little pain but we have improved them to such an extent now that she is able to move around fairly comfortably. Cindy continues to thrive and is obviously enjoying every moment of her life. At Slade House Farm here the foals always give us the most delight and seem to entertain the visitors for us. When Cindy is old enough and when Sue is able to move more freely they will be transferred to one of the other farms where they will spend the rest of their natural lives amongst their friends with all the care and attention they will need. The fact that they are able to do this is due to the observation of one person on a train journey and their effort in actually doing something to help a little donkey in distress.

Sue and Cindy enjoying the garden.

Spider

To almost all animals being in a market is a terrifying experience. Having been uprooted from familiar surroundings, the animal suddenly finds itself surrounded by other terrified animals being herded by blows and shouts. Spider, a four-month-old foal, was put into a West Country market in September 1979 and was surely no exception. He had been transported to market in a large box containing a mixture of horses, ponies and donkeys and up to the time of actually being herded into the pen, had managed to keep fairly close to his mother. However, unfortunately for Spider, his mother was herded into a separate section of the market and poor little Spider found himself alone, being consistently pushed and kicked by the other donkeys with him. Although he brayed pitifully for his mother, and could in fact hear his mother calling out to him, Spider never saw her again from that moment. About four hours later he found himself pushed into a small ring where he was poked and prodded with sticks whilst people began to bid for him.

At this point, Spider's luck began to change, as he was purchased for £28 by the Dartmoor Livestock Protection Society. The society was extremely worried by the conditions in this market, particularly for the young animals which had been abruptly separated from their mothers and were being sold unweaned, and it was only the fact that he went to a knowledgeable home that saved young Spider's life. The same society had previously rescued a donkey called Timothy who had been severely vandalized by having both his ears cut through. They had sent Timothy to us and had been delighted with his amazing recovery. From being so anti-social that he attacked every person and animal in sight, Timothy had settled down with the sanctuary, and the Dartmoor Livestock Protection Society felt sure we could help Spider in a similar way. He was kept by them for approximately five weeks before being sent to the sanctuary. When he arrived he was unnamed and as I walked into the box and saw this pathetic little animal I felt 'Spider' was a suitable name, as his life even then seemed to be hanging on a thread. He was extremely small and weak and his forcible weaning had certainly taken its toll. We immediately set about continuing the skilled care he had been

Spider with his rescuer, 1979; (overleaf) Spider fully recovered.

receiving and this, plus the love and attention he got, soon began to show results.

At about the same time that Spider came in another very poor donkey arrived, so thin we called him 'Bones'. As so often happens at the sanctuary, Spider, Bones and another little donkey called Jenny joined together and made a small group. All the donkeys are wormed on arrival, weighed and thereafter wormed every two months. Parasites are a major problem with donkeys and once the donkey's condition has deteriorated to the extent it had with Spider, Bones and Jenny, it could be disastrous. A careful build-up feeding programme was instigated by the veterinary department and very, very slowly the donkeys began to put on weight. At first Spider had none of the energy normally found in young donkeys of his age, he would stand for hours, head down and eyes dull. Our joy when he began to behave more like a young colt was our reward. His little group had a special care box in the main yard. Each day they were taken out and exercised and the first time Spider found the energy to kick me we all burst out cheering. His friends recovered slightly faster than Spider, so we had to feed them individually to ensure he got his fair share. He loved his bran mash most and we were able to conceal the medication and the badly needed vitamins in the flavour of treacle or molasses. By the spring, the group was sufficiently fit to

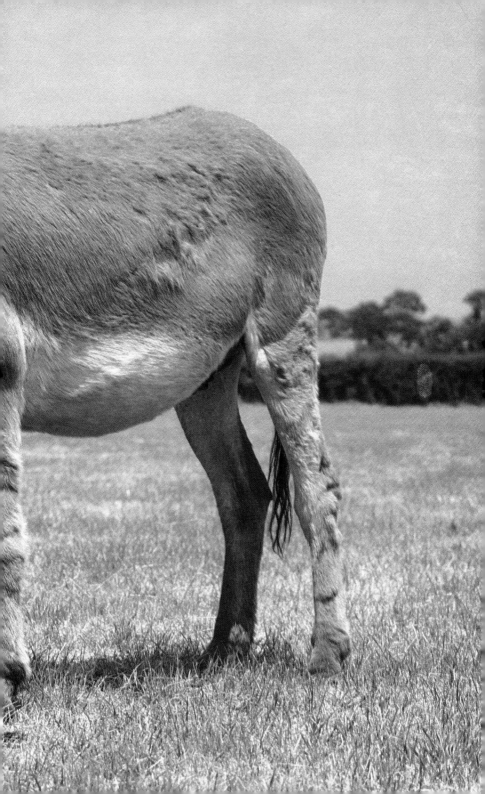

be able to graze outside during the day, although they were always brought in and stabled at night. Spider and his friends had to stay in our special unit at Slade House Farm for over a year before we felt they were fit to be moved at all.

It was decided that the fourth farm the sanctuary purchased would have to be well away from our own locality as we were getting a certain amount of opposition from local farmers who felt we were beginning to take over the area with donkeys, and were becoming a threat to them. John Fry, who had worked with me for many years, set out to find the ideal site within a 40-mile radius. He spent a great deal of time looking at suitable farms but in the end came up with a farm called Three Gates at Leigh in Somerset. Obviously, we had to have a very responsible person to run this as it was so far away from the nucleus and it was agreed that John and his wife Monica should move out there and take over this new, large 192-acre area. There was an immense amount of work to be done when John arrived; some of the fields were very wet, which had made it a rather unproductive farm, and John had to set to work to mole drain many of these to make them suitable as a permanent pasture for the donkeys. Although there were rather more buildings than one would normally find on a farm, we still had to put up an extra large, airy barn as we hoped to have over four hundred donkeys on this farm and it was essential that we had the covered area for the winter quarters. By the time John and his wife and two employees had got the farm prepared, Spider, Bones and Jenny were ready to be moved and so they were among the first donkeys to go out to Three Gates.

There was no doubt that Spider absolutely loved Three Gates. There were over 192 acres and with his two friends he spent many happy days galloping around. He began to develop well and under the careful feeding regime for the underweight donkeys, which consisted of approximately one-fifth of a bale of hay a day and a full handful of special barley nuts in the morning and evening, his coat soon began to shine and he became a very fit and able little donkey. Perhaps because he had lost his mother so early and had become a friend of humans, he always enjoyed following John and his wife around and took a great interest in all the activities of the farm.

Great attention was paid to haymaking as this farm had our biggest potential and, with John's experience, we hoped to make almost sufficient to keep at least Three Gates self-supporting and possibly supply hay to one of the other farms. John was delighted to find early one June morning that the grass was ready to mow and the weather looked set for the next few days; it was with a very happy heart that he mounted the tractor and set off to mow the twelve-acre field.

As always, Spider was leaning over the hedge watching with interest as the mower went past and I have no doubt at all that it was Spider who gave the terrified bray as the baby deer sprang to its feet a second too late as the mower passed. John stopped the machine and ran back absolutely horrified to find that one of the baby deer's legs had been severed just above the knee. Forgetting all thoughts of haymaking he picked up the small terrified animal and ran back to the farmhouse with it. Luckily our vets are always within call and with their skill and the patience and care of John and his wife, 'Bambi', as they called the little deer, survived and made its home in the sanctuary. Although the deer had only three legs it was amazing how it managed to get around and, having lived in the kitchen for the first three or four months, it then moved out into one of the stables and would happily lope along with the donkeys grazing during the day.

Fortunately, no more disasters struck John as he made his hay and the immense amount achieved did in fact help substantially with the costs of the sanctuary and provided all the donkeys with first-class fodder for the winter.

Spider thoroughly enjoyed his first winter at Three Gates. The new barn was quite enormous, it measured 140 feet by 90 feet. Right down the middle of the barn was stored the year's supply of straw and hay which formed a natural separation between the two sides; Spider, Jenny and Bones soon found their own favourite place where they could feed every day. Apart from liberal amounts of hay, they were fed extra nuts during the winter to keep their weight up, and the donkeys were segregated into groups, depending on how much feed John and the veterinary surgeon decided was good for them. I think Spider thoroughly enjoyed being in the maximum feed area and it was quite obvious that he was almost fully recovered from his terrible and drastic start in life when I visited him a short time after he had settled in. Instead of the very quiet, pathetic, almost desperate little creature I had seen some months before, here was a pushy young man who delighted in showing me how quickly he could trot around the concrete yards outside the barn. Every donkey has access to fresh air in the winter and concrete is very good for their hooves as it keeps wearing them down naturally and keeps the foot from softening through standing on the straw bedding.

Jenny soon decided that Bones and Spider were getting a little too much for her and she began to wander off on her own more and more, while Bones and Spider thoroughly enjoyed the pushing and shoving so natural to young geldings of this age. Eventually John

moved Jenny to a group of the older mares where she settled very happily. Spider and Bones, however, just could not wait for the end of the winter and when all the donkeys were let out again in April, they were the first two to gallop out and canter round the fields. I happened to visit the farm very shortly after 'turn-out', as we call it, and the first donkey I noticed was Spider rolling vigorously in the sand heap that we put in every field for them. This sand does two things: firstly, it provides an ideal rolling place for the donkeys, who love to feel the sand rubbing into their coats and backs and obviously it helps in any irritations they may have; secondly, it helps to cure those irritations because we liberally supply the sandpit with delousing powder. For this reason sandpits are to everybody's mutual advantage and when Spider trotted across to me to say 'hello', I almost had to laugh when I patted him, for a great cloud of sand and anti-louse powder rose into the air. I must say as I sat laughing, it was lovely to see Spider throw back his head and give a great bray of delight before galloping off to join Bones. It made my day to see such a happy, healthy little donkey and to think how different his fate could have been following that terrible day in the market.

Bambi at one year old in the hayfield.

Maud and Eyo

One of the biggest problems to the donkey is caused by neglect to its feet. The hoof itself is made of a hard horny material and this needs to be worn down regularly to prevent excessive growth. In the natural state the donkeys tend to move many miles in a day, generally along stony and hard ground, and this provides a natural wear which prevents any problems. However, when donkeys are kept as pets their owners generally put them into a lush field of grass and the donkey has no hard area on which to wear its hooves down. This is perfectly acceptable provided that a farrier attends the donkey every eight weeks and pares down the hoof, filing down any excess to keep the shape of the hoof even.

Unfortunately, many new donkey owners do not realize what great problems the hoof can cause and, either through ignorance or lack of funds, a proper farrier is not employed and the donkey's hooves are allowed to grow. At first the animal can cope with the extended hoof but as it grows longer it becomes misshapen and eventually curls round rather like an Indian slipper; in extreme cases it can make three or four twists and achieve a total length of over 12 inches. This distortion causes great distress to the donkey, affecting its balance and producing a stretching of the tendons which is often irreversible. It is probably fair to say that more prosecutions for cruelty to donkeys are caused by overgrown hooves than any other cause, and special farriers are employed at the sanctuary to cope with this problem.

The owners of Maud and Eyo found themselves in all sorts of problems. Originally they had only wanted one donkey but they were persuaded to accept two by the dealer who sold them and, as they already had one on their limited ground, they found they were totally unable to cope with three animals.

In addition to the problem of feeding, they had not realized that Eyo was a stallion and, during the course of the year they were together, Maud, who was approximately fifteen years old, was put into foal. Luckily the owners discussed their problem with a local stud farm and the owner there recommended that the best way to try and solve the problem would be to send the donkeys to the

Maud on arrival at the sanctuary.

Donkey Sanctuary. And so in June 1982 Maud and Eyo arrived. By this time their feet were at a critical stage, where, in the case of Maud, permanent crippling seemed inevitable. Up to a short time ago the policy of both veterinary surgeons and farriers was to remove a little of the hoof each week and allow the tendons to gradually tighten up, giving the donkey a chance to adjust to a new method of balancing, and this is how Maud was treated. The current recommendation is to remove the unwanted hoof as soon as possible, but this has to be extremely carefully supervised by both a veterinary surgeon and a farrier with a special knowledge of this technique. Today's farriers are being trained in this method and it would seem from recent cases admitted to the sanctuary that this does not cause the difficulties that such drastic action had previously been thought to cause. Great care must always be taken to see that the balance of the foot is maintained.

Both Maud and Eyo were very kind, gentle donkeys and were isolated together while their feet were attended. However, Maud appeared in a great deal of distress and after two days we decided that they would have to be put in the special box that we use when stallions and mares come in together. This is a large, long airy box separated down the middle by wooden bars so that Maud and Eyo could talk to each other through the bars, but each had a certain

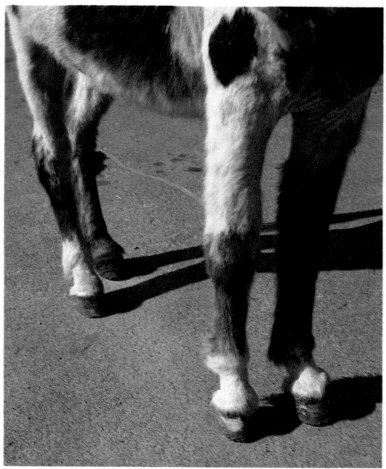

Maud's feet today after two years of care; (opposite) Maud and Eyo with Paul.

amount of privacy. Eyo of course, being a stallion, would have to be castrated as soon as he was strong enough and his feet were in a better condition, and Maud, although at this stage we were not sure she was pregnant, certainly appeared to be in a lot of discomfort. In fact, I was so worried about her that I set up a two-hour night watch between myself and Jane MacNeill, our current vet at that time. On the Saturday following their arrival I went in to see Maud at 10 in the evening, Jane went in at midnight and 2 a.m., and on each of the visits everything seemed perfectly in order. To my horror, when I went in at 4 o'clock in the morning, I found Maud lying down in deep distress with a tiny, half-formed foal beside her. I could have wept, that poor little Maud had gone through such a bad time, and I really felt that we had rescued her too late. I ran to get Jane and, with her expert medical help, we were able to save Maud's life, but we both looked sadly at the pathetic little bundle in the corner, for which any form of help was impossible. Maud recovered fairly rapidly from the abortion but her feet continued giving her trouble and she stayed at Slade House Farm in the intensive care unit for over twelve months. As soon as Eyo had been castrated he rejoined her and they were both able to take it very easy, as use was gradually restored to their legs.

One of the most difficult problems was persuading Maud to walk. Her feet had hurt for so long that she seemed to have built up a psychological barrier to exercise. After her abortion on medical grounds she just *had* to keep moving and a new piece of equipment we had just purchased became invaluable. We adapted this machine, commonly known as a 'horse walker', to a 'donkey walker'. A circular strip of concrete is laid and a pivot is placed in the middle, from which long arms extend, and the donkey's lead rein is attached to an arm. Behind each donkey is a second arm with a rubber flap on it. The motor is turned on, and the 'arm' leads the donkey along. If the donkey slows or stops, the rubber flap gently propels the donkey from behind. Should the donkey stop altogether and dig his or her heels in, the machine is stopped. Maud and Eyo were put on the exerciser and received the greatest benefit from it. To start with Maud was in front and Eyo followed happily, but Maud kept tripping over as she tried to look over her shoulder to see Eyo. The solution was to harness each donkey opposite the other and then, with the odd bray of communication, they exercised happily half an hour a day.

By the time Maud and Eyo were ready to go out to one of the farms, we had just purchased our fifth unit. We had taken a long time finding the site; East Devon is especially beautiful and is very good for dairy farming and, as well as not wishing to take good land from farmers, we also knew that donkeys thrive better on more second-class land, and so we were looking for an area within reach of the sanctuary but slightly below the grade one farming area. We found the ideal situation at Tedburn St Mary, close to Dartmoor, where a farm came up for sale which seemed suitable in many ways. Although close to the village, the fields ran clear to the west, and the accommodation for the donkeys was ideal. Apart from the home farm buildings, which consisted of large stable blocks around a central square courtyard, there were large, airy barns up a separate track away from the village and these seemed to be ideal units to use for wintering the donkeys. My son Paul, who had been so helpful with the donkeys in his younger days, had returned from six years in the Air Force a year previously and expressed a desire to come and work again for the sanctuary. He had received 12 months' experience at Slade House Farm and the other farms, where all the managers had helped and been as co-operative as they could and, with his basic love of the donkey, and his eagerness to learn, he seemed ideal as the fifth farm manager. Paul and his wife, Ushi, moved out to Town Barton and began the enormous job of getting it ready for its influx of donkeys. The farm itself has 152 acres and this meant over 6 miles of fencing. The cost of fencing is quite enormous and Paul and his newly employed team began the long job on their own, and seemed to work miracles within a very short time.

At that time the intake of donkeys into the sanctuary had increased to over six a week, and we were becoming overcrowded on all the farms. So, as soon as Paul and his team had got one of the large barns cleaned out, sterilized with steam cleaning and all set up with clean straw and hay for the donkeys, with the adjoining field fenced, the first group of donkeys was selected for Town Barton. It is always an exciting day when a new farm receives its first intake, and two of the first donkeys on the lorry to go were Maud and Eyo. What a difference there was in these two little donkeys as they jauntily trotted up the ramp, when I recalled their arrival and their agonizing, slow walk down the ramp to their new quarters; I could scarcely believe that they were the same two donkeys. The lorry, which with all the partitions removed, can take between 12 and 15 at a time, was loaded up throughout the day and over 6 trips were made. By 6 p.m. that evening 72 donkeys had taken up residence at Town Barton and the tired and happy group of us stood watching them walk around their new, large, airy barn, enjoying, as donkeys always do, new surroundings and exploring every inch of the beautiful new pasture that was available for them.

Maud and Eyo set off together and both were able to break into a trot as they surveyed their new field. They seemed rather dis-

appointed that they could not get their heads far enough through the fence to nibble the hedge. They always seem to enjoy eating through the bars and we have to be careful when fencing to keep the fence far enough away to protect the hedge, so useful to wildlife and as a windbreak. Maud and Eyo decided we had got it right and regretfully trotted to the bottom of the field to see if there was any way they could paddle in the stream. Once again they were thwarted, but seemed pleased enough with their new home as they returned to the barn to sample the straw bedding, so lovingly and deeply laid for them.

Over the next few months the whole farm was fenced, and special shelters built at strategic places on the farm. The total number of donkeys to be cared for at Town Barton will eventually be in the region of four hundred and so great care had to be taken in planning where the shelters should be placed. Paul wanted these built in concrete so that they could serve as winter as well as summer quarters, and each was designed with a series of gates and tracks leading into three different big field areas. This meant that fields could be rested while the donkeys, still using the same shelter, had a track to another field which was ready for use. This rotation method allows the farm to be used with the minimum number of buildings.

Maud and Eyo have now settled in happily to a group consisting of the original 72 who arrived together, and it is hard to tell, as they gallop from shelter to field, that they have ever been in such terrible trouble. Let us hope they will have many happy years of life before them and, with constant care from the farrier, their foot problems should be a thing of the past.

Happy together at last.

Zorba the Greek

In a large part of the world the donkey plays a vital role in the economy and often this can mean a life of extremely hard work, discomfort and sometimes even physical cruelty being inflicted on the animal. Realizing the problems, I started a charity some time ago called the International Donkey Protection Trust, whose aims and objects are to alleviate cruelty and suffering to donkeys and mules in all parts of the world.

I have certainly seen some terrible sights, but I have been heartened in many instances to find that the poverty-stricken owner of the donkey does care for his animal to the best of his ability, and very often the donkey's needs are met as well as those of the peasant's children. This is of course because, without the donkey, the peasant has no means of gaining an income. The donkey's work starts very early in the morning and consists of many and varying jobs from ploughing, carrying essential water for the family, firewood, animal feed, food supplies and goods to the markets.

Our unexpected arrival at many villages from North Africa to South America has always been most warmly received. We have set up small clinics and dealt with untold numbers of sores and injuries, advised the peasants on the maximum load their donkeys should take, and helped them in re-designing the packs they use for carrying to prevent terrible sores being repeated. I also put pressure on the relevant government to improve the situation.

In many Arab countries, the situation for donkeys is disastrous. In Egypt, for example, I have seen donkeys at the point of death from emaciation and exhaustion, being cruelly beaten by their owners as they try their best to drag heavy carts, laden with refuse and humans up the five-mile hill from Cairo to the refuse area in the Mokattam hills. On the refuse tips live the Zabalin Community, their owners.

I always take great trouble to age all the donkeys I treat. This is done by looking at the teeth and is really quite simple once one has become experienced. I was surprised to find that in the poorer communities I very rarely found a donkey over the age of eleven. When we were able to obtain assistance from local veterinary surgeons, who normally never bother with donkeys as their owners have no means of paying them, I found that they were equally amazed that I thought a donkey should live longer than eleven years of age. As one of them said to me, 'How long do you expect a cat to live in your country?' and when I said approximately sixteen years, he then replied, 'Well, eleven years is the age of the donkey.' I did, however, know from experience at the sanctuary that the average life expectancy of our donkeys is thirty-seven years and there seemed a tremendous difference here, an important difference when the donkeys were so desperately needed by the poor people and were in so many cases almost members of the family. On our tours I began to take a small laboratory as I suspected the cause of deaths could be too many parasites and it appears that this first premiss was correct. Obviously, three weeks in a foreign country is not sufficient time to test or to prove any idea and so we decided to set up a trial in Greece where we were receiving great co-operation from both the Ministry of Agriculture and the Agricultural Bank of Greece. We chose three islands to work on, taking 30 animals on Kea and Paros each, and 40 on Crete, so 100 animals were in the trial, and began a two-year project of dosing and treating for parasites.

Zorba was a stallion who lived on the island of Kea. Kea is a small island to be found almost due east of Athens and is reached by ferryboat from the harbour of Lavrio. Zorba was one of the strongest and fittest donkeys on the island, the main reason being that his owner worked as an assistant to the veterinary surgeon there, called Stratos Grosomanidis. Zorba was a very large, well built donkey and he served as stallion for almost all the matings on the island; this important role meant that he was rather specially cared for and did perhaps a little less work than the other donkeys on Kea. He lived in a small village at the top of a mountain. In the early days the village had been sited down by the harbour, but after a series of raids by pirates many years ago, the whole village was removed and built almost 6 kilometres up the hillside. It really is the most delightful village, entered through a very narrow archway, which was easy to defend, and spreading on a series of cobbled terraces up the side of the mountain. Very few cars go to the village and almost all the transport is by donkey or mule. Zorba's friends, living in Santorini, have a hard life when the cruise ships come in. Often up to 600 passengers are carried by donkeys/mules up the 800 steps to Thira, the town. Fortunately, a cable car has now been installed, but even so, many overweight tourists think it 'more fun' to ride up on the donkey.

(Overleaf) *Zorba awaiting treatment at the veterinary surgery.*

Zorba's quarters were a very small, dark shed only yards from the house of his owner, the door of which opened directly on to the narrow alleyway which provided access to the village. He enjoyed the cool darkness which helped to prevent the flies which pestered him constantly when standing outside. During the summer, the temperature was frequently between 30–35°C, but, by contrast, winter could be cold and very windy. Zorba's normal day would begin very early in the morning between 5.30 a.m. and 6 a.m., when he would be taken round the small outlying houses to collect the milk which had been produced and bring it back to a communal tank which stood on the edge of the village. After this he would be taken down to the dock where he would be loaded with goods to bring back up to the village, and the rest of his day would then consist of carrying loads from house to house.

However, Zorba's day altered quite dramatically early in May 1981. On this day, instead of his usual panniers being placed on his back, he was led down by his owner to the veterinary surgeon's office which was halfway down the hill. There, with twenty-nine other donkeys, he stood patiently waiting whilst a large group of strange people began the most unusual task. At first he almost disgraced himself as the tape measure was passed around his midriff to measure his girth; it tickled so much he almost broke away from his owner. Then he stood more quietly as his heart rate was taken and his lungs listened to through a stethoscope. Probably he had never had such a thorough examination in his life, even down to his feet being picked up and examined. We had, of course, been expecting the usual poor-grade donkeys that we had seen in many other parts of the world and our team had arrived to take dung samples which were carefully analysed by the laboratories run by the Greek Ministry of Agriculture and by ourselves, and to dose the donkeys with an anthelmintic manufactured by Pfizer and supplied to us at a very special price, which got rid of worms. I just couldn't believe my eyes when I saw Zorba. He really was one of the most magnificent donkeys I have seen either here, in a show ring, or anywhere else in the world, and we were delighted to grade him number five, which was our best grade for any donkey, and also to be given the opportunity to make the best stallion on the island parasite-free. His owner, Kiriakos Korandis, was rightly very proud of Zorba and was delighted to have his photograph taken with him. Zorba quite enjoyed the anthelmintic taste. The main diet of donkeys on Kea, as in many other parts of the world, is alfalfa grass which obviously does not have the same pepperminty taste as the medicine we were dosing the donkeys with.

Working with our team, and in fact the most vital part of the team perhaps, was a Greek veterinary surgeon, Iannis Georgoulakis, a parasitologist who had done his PhD in the USA. He had been supplied by the Agricultural Bank of Greece to help us and spoke excellent English. We decided to find out more about Zorba's work as we were all so impressed with this magnificent animal. Zorba's owner told us that one of the big problems on the island was a means of income and their greatest worry was the amount of milk they produced, for which they had no market. Iannis was quick to find a way whereby the Agricultural Bank of Greece would help these hard-working people, and he immediately put plans in hand for a small dairy to be set up; during the course of our two years' work we were delighted to see this dairy built and the milk produce increased to 5,000 litres per day. The islanders now have a new source of income as a tanker arrives at least twice a week from the mainland and collects the milk from the dairy. Zorba now found his job altered slightly in that he no longer brought the milk back from the local producers to the village, but took it direct to the dairy; he and over thirty other donkeys now have regular employment performing this task.

Although Zorba had been in excellent condition when we first went, it was marvellous to see the immense improvement in his condition after the two years of our treatment. His coat began to shine, his energy appeared unbounded and we heard that his performance with all the mares had improved beyond all expectation. The other donkeys in the group, some of whom had started as low as grade two, were rapidly improving and at the end of the two-year period there was no doubt at all, even to the inexperienced eye, that those donkeys in the trial who had been receiving the treatment were substantially better than those who had not had the treatment. A paper has now been published on the whole trial, substantiated by the veterinary surgeons involved and the parasitologist, which will be given as much publicity as possible, as I feel this is a real way to help the Third World. In our opinion if governments could subsidize this simple dosing programme in their very poor areas, then they would help not only the donkeys – whose general health improves out of all recognition – but also the very poor peasant owners. When the peasant's donkey dies it is similar to us having a car written off and to many of these very poor people it can prove the final straw. So as we improve the donkey's health and longevity, we would also improve the people's lot.

In view of the excellent results from Kea, we decided to continue dosing after two years and to extend it to every equine on the island, as we felt it would be extremely interesting and valuable to have a whole area, small though it be, in the world, where we could control

Zorba loaded with his owner.

parasites and see the general improvement in both condition and longevity of the donkey.

In June 1984 we visited Kea with a film crew and filmed Zorba with his friends and, whilst in Greece, we were delighted when the Deputy Governor of the Agricultural Bank of Greece announced in the film that as a result of our work and the knowledge that the economic losses caused by worm infestation in animals were enormous, the Greek government had allocated 150 million drachmas for treatment of parasites for agricultural animals, and from next year donkeys would be included. This was wonderful news for us, and for Zorba it means he seems well set for the future and for many years will be receiving his pepperminty dose.

Joey Clews

As my whole life is now devoted to donkeys, I spend a great deal of time in conversation about these delightful animals with members of the general public. Almost without exception, at some stage of the conversation people recount to me their earliest recollections of donkeys and, in almost every case, this was the pleasure of donkey rides given when they were young children. Those happy memories, which combine the fun and pleasure of a holiday with the thrill and excitement to a young child of a donkey ride, make a great impression, and I am quite sure that Joey Clews, during the many years he spent on Blackpool Beach, has given enormous pleasure to countless children.

It is not always realized how many donkeys work on beaches in this country and it may be interesting to know that during 1983 there were 63 licensed beach operators working, which means over 1,000 donkeys at work. With the exception of Blackpool, every beach operator has to satisfy the local authorities that he is a suitable person to run the beach franchise, that he has a good knowledge of his donkeys' needs, the tack they are to use, and is willing to co-operate with the requirements of the licensing body. The Donkey Sanctuary Inspectorate play an important role in the procedure of licensing. A veterinary surgeon does the annual inspection and during this inspection every animal is checked carefully from a health point of view and all the tack examined to make sure it fits correctly and is in good condition. Once the licence has been granted, our inspectors visit the beaches regularly to ensure that the regulations laid down regarding the weights which donkeys can carry (a maximum of 8 stone) and the permitted hours of work (nine) for the donkey are being complied with. In addition, the donkeys must be fed and watered at midday and, if our inspectors find any breach of the regulations, they can go back to the local council, who are in a position to revoke the licence if they feel there are sufficient grounds.

The Blackpool regulations are slightly different from those in other parts of the country. This is because Blackpool has always been very, very conscious of the value of the beach donkeys to its

(Above and opposite) *Typical beach donkeys.*

tourist trade and it was over a hundred years ago that they drew up their Donkey Charter. This is similar in requirements to those of other local councils but in addition Blackpool has built some wonderful stabling where the donkeys can rest after their work in almost ideal conditions. Because of the length of the beach and the obviously popular sites for the donkey riding, the operators are given a different site during each week in rotation. This system is fair to both owners and donkeys, as some weeks the donkeys are very busy on the pitches near the Tower and the Piers, whereas on other weeks they have a more restful time away from the main popular area. The sanctuary has had a very good working relationship with the beach operators for many years and a previous inspector, Inspector Matthews of the RSPCA, liaised with the sanctuary on many occasions to ensure that retiring donkeys came down to the Donkey Sanctuary in Devon.

Joey Clews came into this category just before Christmas 1983. His owner decided to retire him as he had reached twenty years of age, and with his typical concern for the donkeys, contacted us immediately he had arranged the winter quarters for his herd, as he realized that, once all the other donkeys had gone, Joey would be very lonely left on his own.

Due to the length of the journey, Perry, the driver, made an

overnight stop. This enabled Joey to stretch his legs and put in some good eating time, without the motion of the lorry distracting him. Because he was so large he was given two sections of the box, and when he arrived we were pleased to see how well he had travelled. Unloading him was no problem, and he walked down the ramp in an extremely calm and composed manner. We were amazed to see that he was almost as big as Buffalo, one of our donkeys who had also worked on Blackpool Beach and who, in fact, had known Joey for many years. Joey also had an enormous set of ears and was a very well built donkey, with the kindest gentlest nature possible. They say that nature has endowed the donkey with big ears and a large voice for a special reason. In the days when both horses and donkeys ran wild and were not used by man, the horse with its superior strength maintained possession of the more fertile valleys, chasing away the smaller donkey up the sides of the hills, and so the donkey learned to browse on poorer pasture than that enjoyed by the horse. As the donkeys had to scatter over large areas to find their food up the hillsides and mountains they developed large ears which could turn to locate their fellow equines across very large areas. The voice was used for the same purpose. I think there must

(Overleaf) *Joey beginning to lose his winter coat.*

be a great deal of truth in this as just occasionally, when the wind is in the right direction, the donkeys on our farm at Paccombe almost two miles away can hear the donkeys on the farm at Slade here, and a good deal of vocal practice takes place, proving the theory.

Joey settled very quickly on his arrival. Following a complete and thorough veterinary examination, he was given his combined anti-flu and anti-tetanus innoculations, had his feet cared for, and was checked to make sure that he had no specific problems. He was in very good health indeed and there were no special foot or lice problems, which we so often find with other intake donkeys, and at the end of the four-week isolation period, Joey was ready to go and join a group.

Normally, the donkeys that come in stay with the admission group that they have been with during their isolation period, but we decided that it would be rather nice if Joey could join the group of donkeys from Blackpool that he had not seen for seven years at their little unit on Slade House Farm. By this time Buffalo was thirty-seven years old, a reasonable average for a donkey who has been well cared for and treated well all his life, but quite an achievement for Buffalo who had obviously worked very, very hard for a long period of time. Some donkeys have problems with their lungs and because Buffalo had been having some discomfort, his particular little group had been allocated a large airy shed which was bedded with peat. This prevented any excess dust which irritated his lungs, whilst providing a nice soft place for the more elderly animals to lie. Putting Joey on a halter, we led him along the track to what was to be his new home.

One is always careful when introducing a new animal to a group as there could be some pushing or biting and so, as was our usual practice, we stopped alongside the enclosure and let the donkeys talk to each other over the wooden fence. It really was quite amazing. Although these animals had not seen each other for seven years, there was an immediate rapport. Buffalo and Bobby seemed to know that it was a friend that had arrived and there were the most enormous and delightful brays of welcome. After two minutes' talking over the fence, it was apparent that there was to be no biting or kicking on this meeting, and so we opened the gate and led Joey in. The scenes that followed were almost indescribable. Each donkey appeared ecstatic and they all rolled together in the peat, kicking up their legs, trotted around the concrete enclosure, braying almost non-stop for nearly ten minutes. After this time, with Bobby on one side and Buffalo on the other, Joey was escorted round his new home, and the obvious pleasure the three took in being together was most touching.

We always take particular pleasure in taking in donkeys that have spent their lives working on the beach; after they have given so much pleasure to so many children, I feel it is a far better fate for the donkeys than to be sent to a market where not only are they terrified, but often land up after days of travelling at a slaughter-house; I really do feel that they deserve more than this. The donkeys coming in from the beaches are always extremely sociable and it is interesting to stand and watch in the fields in the summer as their natural instinct when they see children by the fence is to walk across to talk to them. When the handicapped children from the Slade Centre ride past up the drive on one of their circuits, the donkeys who trot across, stand to watch and often bray, are generally ex-beach donkeys and this delightful side of the donkey's nature is one of their most endearing features.

Many beach donkeys are *not* so lucky. We are frequently called to cases where mares who have recently foaled are being used, their foal either left in desperate condition at home, or, almost worse, penned in on the beach for the public to admire. Obviously, they are a good crowd puller, and at least they are re-united with their mothers at the break times, but neither should be there at all, and we strongly oppose this method of exploitation. Some operators allow the young boys and girls running the rides to use sticks, or even worse, electric goads. These prod the already tired donkeys to force them to exceed their natural pace, and once again, we oppose the use of such horrors.

In the spring of 1984 a great deal of publicity was received by a beach operator when he was given notice his licence would not be renewed. He had been giving rides for many years and for hygenic reasons his licence was stopped. Despite offers from many people, including us, to take the donkeys, great headlines appeared in the press 'Beach donkeys to be slaughtered'. We received over 140 calls and letters within 24 hours of the article appearing. I'm always warmed by the concern of the public and am delighted they know whom to contact. We were already in the picture through an inspector there, so we were able to reassure all the callers that we hoped the donkeys were in no danger, having been offered sanctuary here.

Winter quarters for beach donkeys often give us cause for concern; once again Joey was lucky to have wintered in Blackpool. Donkeys at Weston-super-Mare up to 1980 were forced to winter by the local tip on reclaimed land originally a rubbish dump. Each evening they waited patiently until a gate in the fence was opened and they then fed on the council rubbish dump for the night. We made approaches to the Environmental Department of the Weston-

super-Mare Council, and, after receiving little response, publicized the donkeys' plight through our Newsletter. The response of our supporters was magnificent and the pressure put on the council soon resulted in the donkeys being moved.

For Joey, Buffalo and Bobby, their future is secure. They will have the company of their friends and of children for the rest of their natural days, and we hope that they will be joined by many more ex-beach friends in the future.

Printed below is a simplification of the regulations relating to working donkeys:

Every donkey must have at least one hour's rest midday for watering and feeding, plus other short rests, and NEVER stay on the beach more than nine hours in a day.

No one over 8 stones may ride a donkey.

Mare with young foals should not work.

No sticks should be used.

Joey rejoins his group of friends.

George

We first heard about George in July 1980. He had been rescued by a vicar living near Windsor, who, to put it mildly, had been sadly misled over the needs of the donkey. When he bought the donkey, to save it from slaughter, he was told that he only needed the feet done twice a year (whereas they should be trimmed every couple of months) and to give it two scoops of pony nuts a day (whereas in winter a donkey needs much more than this). No mention was made of the amount of land needed to keep the donkey (which is a minimum of half an acre), worming or the need for shelter, adequate fencing, nor the fact that single donkeys do tend to get very lonely and therefore that it is best to keep two. Despite great care from the vicar and his family, George became difficult and a call for help was made to the sanctuary. It was our field inspector who made the first inspection. She immediately realized that George was very lonely and this was the reason for the problems his owners were experiencing; unfortunately, as they didn't have sufficient acreage, it was impossible to suggest that he had a friend to live with him, which would have solved the problem. She had no option but to recommend that he came into the sanctuary. The family were very concerned as they felt they had failed George in some way and they were genuinely sad and unhappy to see him go. However, the fact that he was coming to the sanctuary where he could possibly be trained to work with the disabled children at the Slade Centre was some consolation.

George arrived with the usual characteristics of donkeys who have been on their own – he was aggressive, difficult to handle, objected vigorously to being handled or even petted, and brayed frequently – but in a very short time he had settled down. We had been advised that he was about 11 years old but we are able to age donkeys very accurately here by their teeth and he was in fact correctly aged at almost 22. This made him too old to be suitable for training at the Slade Centre and for two years he joined the group of donkeys known as 'Boys Group' at Brookfield Farm. As well as helping donkeys who are in trouble our inspectors also have the job of following up requests from people to re-home a donkey and this

George

again is an important part of the Donkey Sanctuary's work. We feel that gelding donkeys, once they have settled down with us and got over any problems they may have had before they joined us, can only benefit from being part of a small family rather than a large group, and as the average cost of keeping a donkey each week at the sanctuary is approximately £11.00 we are always on the lookout for really good, suitable homes. At this time, only gelding donkeys were being rehomed. Mares had a tendency to be 'accidentally' got into foal and of course stallions were difficult to handle and could increase our problems by putting local mares into foal. We have the most stringent rules regarding the new 'foster owners' and the inspector's job is to visit the proposed homes; there they go through a long checklist to ensure that there is adequate grazing, fencing, field shelters, water supply and, even more important, to ensure that the foster parents are fully aware of the donkey's needs and feeding requirements. Provided all this is satisfactory then a special form is signed which legally ensures that the donkey is still the property of the Donkey Sanctuary and has a right to return at any time, and that the interests of the donkey are to come first at all times. In the event of the home finding it difficult to provide adequate funds should the donkey become ill and require veterinary treatment, then the sanctuary also agrees to see that this is covered. The inspector then arranges for the donkeys in question to be delivered to their new home, is there when they arrive and the new owners are given a complete history of the donkeys to date with all their likes and dislikes and as much background as possible and also a folder so that a diary can be kept of the inspector's visits. These take place regularly every three months; if at any of those visits the inspector is dissatisfied with the donkeys' condition, then the sanctuary has the right to take them back.

After two years George was completely settled at Brookfield: a good strong donkey but one who obviously liked individual attention and was always following the managers around. Because of this and his excellent condition, as well as the fact that he had made no particular friend and seemed to prefer humans, George was put up for consideration when a very good home was offered at Chiselborough in Somerset. There were already two horses, called Breeze and Rocky, and in view of the fact that before George had been rescued by the vicar he had been in with a group of five horses, we decided he could possibly be tried in this new home. Mrs Cade, who offered the home, had been in contact with us for some time and was obviously a very knowledgeable person and had been a contributor to the Donkey Sanctuary for several years. She was very interested in the Slade Centre and had promised to raise funds specifically for that project. Having received a most enthusiastic report from our inspector, Mr Judge, we sent George to Chiselborough, where he caused great changes for everybody.

With an owner who thoroughly enjoyed taking George out for walks, they soon became a regular sight walking together through the lanes of Somerset. Mrs Cade being well under eight stone, she decided she would like to ride George and wrote to the vicar to enquire if George had previously been ridden or driven. The vicar was delighted to hear from the new owner and see that George was doing so well and in fact sent a copy of the parish magazine which contained an article on George in his new home. On the front he wrote 'by very tortuous investigations (via the pub!) I find George has been ridden – quite a long time ago – but not driven.' Mrs Cade then rang up our inspector to enquire about riding and driving, and was told as long as she was under eight stone and she trained George properly there would be no problem with either. The earlier

In his prize-winning hat.

86

walks and commands he had learnt, such as 'stop', 'walk on', 'trot', 'stand' and 'no', stood him in good stead. A donkey does not need to be 'broken' and will usually allow rides to anyone of a suitable weight without fuss.

The riding skills required by the rider are exactly those for a pony, but extra care must be taken with the saddle, which must have a crupper. A donkey has almost no withers and without the crupper (a strap from the back of the saddle with a loop around the donkey's tail), the saddle would slip forward. Many donkeys join riding classes in local shows and can even complete hurdle races with great credit. Young members of hunts occasionally join on well trained donkeys and once the horses are used to the strange participant, they take little notice. Mrs Cade and George developed the most wonderful relationship and I quote from her letter with regard to Chiselborough Fête which gives some idea of the pleasure that they were each obtaining from the other.

George had his greatest success so far on 10th July at Chiselborough Fête, when he entered the Pet Show and Fancy Hat competition. With regard to the latter, we tried on the hat unadorned first (ear holes cut out) to see if it would worry George at all. He appeared to love it, and so it was trimmed. It was an imitation straw, black, with floppy brim. When George moved his ears the brim fell forward, and although this looked rather rakish it no doubt partially obstructed his vision. We folded back the brim, and white lace was sewn all round, with a lace rose on top of the crown and a beige rose in front. George wore it all afternoon, and when my husband, Eric, took him back to the paddock, he said George was reluctant to have the hat removed!

As I was in the tea tent all afternoon washing up, Clare, aged 13, took George in to the Pet Show and Eric in to the Fancy Hat competition. George won first prize – a lovely red rosette – for being the best behaved animal in the show. As he was competing with dogs, cats, rabbits, guinea pigs, gerbils and tortoises we are wondering how the behaviour of the tortoises was judged! Apparently the pet show was next to the coconut shy and George stood by this with sounds like cannon balls exploding around him, without turning a hair. For the Fancy Hat competition Eric had to lead George round and round with the Stoke Silver Band in full blast. Here George was given 50p and instructions not to fritter it away on ginger biscuits!

The very generous paddock in which George was kept was almost his undoing, however, as donkeys do tend to eat more than they require and George began to get fatter and fatter and his stomach began to sag and sag until a comment of 'When is she due to foal?' persuaded Mrs Cade that the time had come to slim him down again. George was put on stricter rations. The apples in the orchard did cause one or two problems. Mrs Cade used to pick the apples by climbing up onto the loose box roof via a ladder and one day while she was rather perilously picking, she heard a terrible clatter and, looking down, saw George had knocked away the metal ladder. He was standing looking at her in some amazement sitting on top of the roof and as she knew the baker was due in 40 minutes, Mrs Cade felt the situation was rather embarrassing. Luckily for her, a friend called round in the nick of time, the ladder was replaced and dignity restored.

By October 1982 it was decided that George should be trained to pull a small cart. The many walks on the roads had provided good background training and a beautiful little float with side seats and a door at the back with a step up was purchased. By May of the following year basic training was over and they were both able to set off with a reasonable chance of a relaxing drive. To help the Slade Centre, an impressive open day, named Fiesta, is held every second year. Over 6,000 people attend and generally at least £3,000 net profit is made. Large colourful Fiesta posters are printed and Mrs Cade pinned one of these on the back of the cart and made a practice of going out on the B3165 every Saturday morning. As she said, this gave George practice with heavy traffic and, as they had to stay behind for some time, drivers had plenty of opportunity to read the Fiesta poster.

By this time Mrs Cade had joined the Donkey Breed Society and so she went to the Bath and West Show to watch the donkeys and the driving. She was interested to compare the brays heard here with those of George because by now she was getting complaints from the villagers that they hadn't heard George braying, as apparently the whole village used to enjoy this. Mrs Cade wrote regularly to us with many amusing incidents with regard to our dear George and we were most amused to hear that one day, proceeding sedately along the B3165, they rounded a corner to find a combine harvester advancing towards them. The driver sensibly stopped and turned off his engine; George apparently also stopped and turned off his engine and totally refused to move either forwards or back, which caused an immediate traffic jam. Mrs Cade, realizing an impasse had been reached, gave George a flick with the whip on his

(Overleaf) *Ready to go in the adventure cart.*

shoulder, and – whether from outrage or astonishment – George moved forward immediately. As Mrs Cade says, she admits there wasn't much room to pass but didn't think George really needed to attempt to scale the bank. However, eventually everything was straightened out again and as they passed the cavalcade behind the combine, one man put his head out of the window and said, 'That was well worth waiting for'. Apparently George and owner drove on with heads held high.

This road seemed to be their bête noire, as, on a further occasion, just when Mrs Cade thought she had met all road hazards possible, she found she had overlooked pneumatic drills. Rounding a corner, they came across a team of men repairing the road with a pneumatic drill going full blast. George came to a sudden halt and the operator very kindly stopped too. However, just after the float had passed, the pneumatic drill started again and, according to Mrs Cade, 'George shot forward like a kangaroo and this activity continued most of the way up Norton High Street'. Frequent letters from Mrs Cade, all amusing, go to show us how many people are helping the donkeys. Regular visits and reports from our inspectors show that George is not alone among the three hundred re-homed donkeys to be thoroughly enjoying his new life. Not only does he have everything he needs but he also has the knowledge that a permanent future is guaranteed should he ever find himself in problems with his current owner. One has to remember that the average life expectancy of the donkey appears to be around thirty-seven years old and this does mean that many donkeys going to apparently good homes are going to outlive their owners and donkeys are going to continue getting into trouble for many years to come. However, our long term policy of not breeding and trying to re-home animals must surely eventually get to grips with the problem.

By the same author

DOWN AMONG THE DONKEYS

EEYORE AND THE BROKEN COLLAR

TANSY'S RESCUE

EEYORE HELPS A BADGER

THE GREAT ESCAPE

TWELVE OF MY FAVOURITE DONKEYS

THE STORY OF EEYORE, THE NAUGHTIEST DONKEY IN THE
SANCTUARY

THE DONKEYS CHRISTMAS SURPRISE

THE STORY OF SUEY, THE BEACH DONKEY

MORE ADVENTURES OF EEYORE

EEYORE HELPS THE CHILDREN

JACKO, THE HURRICANE DONKEY

EEYORE AND CHRISTMAS CRACKERS

(Overleaf) *Happy donkeys grazing at Slade House Farm.*